GW00992183

MESSIAH

5

Five Jewish people
make the greatest discovery

JOHN RITCHIE LTD
CHRISTIAN PUBLICATIONS

40 Beansburn, Kilmarnock, Scotland

Contents

Introduction

Now, as never before, with uncertainty the only certainty in our modern world, many Jewish people are searching for their roots and looking for their promised Messiah. Here, in this fascinating book, are five true stories of Jewish people who sought for and discovered the true identity of the Coming One.

CHAPTER 1

Walking Back To Happiness

Helen Shapiro
London, England

I was raised in a warm, musical, traditional Jewish family in the heart of a large Jewish community in Hackney, in the East End of London. Our extended family, although not a very orthodox group, was nevertheless totally Jewish in identity and heritage.

My first recollections include wonderful annual festivals such as Passover, plus traditional rituals such as the lighting of candles on a Friday evening to welcome Shobbes (Shabbat). I believed in God from my earliest days. I took His existence for granted. The State school I attended taught the Bible and I loved the Bible stories very much. However, because my school had a Jewish Headmaster and a large Jewish contingency among the pupils, we Jewish kids had separate R.E. (religious education) classes and assemblies. As a consequence, I never heard of a New Testament or of Jesus until I was around six years of age. One day, a non-Jewish girl came up to me in the playground in quite some distress and blurted out, *"You killed Jesus Christ!"* I was devastated and confused by this accusation. I had never killed anyone in my life, and who was this person with the strange name - Jesus Christ? At 14, while still at school, I had my first hit record. That led me into show business, travelling the world, singing at many famous venues and having more hit songs, including 'Walking Back to

4

Happiness'. I was carried along by all the fame, meeting celebrities and royalty and didn't give much thought to spiritual things until the late 1960's. At that time, it seemed that everyone was searching for the 'meaning of life'. It was the 'hippie' era.

Thankfully, I did not become involved with drugs or cults. However, members of my family had taken to visiting mediums and clairvoyants to make contact (as they thought) with relatives who had died. Having always had a curiosity about life-after-death issues, this fascinated me. I began to visit such people myself, on occasions. I also started reading books and magazines about spiritism, Buddhism and all kinds of psychic phenomena. I developed a system of beliefs, over the years, which incorporated a little bit of this and a little bit of that - a smorgasbord of 'isms' which, these days, would be called 'New Age'. To my own way of thinking, I was not remotely involved in anything evil. I associated everything I believed in with God.

For quite a number of years, I was comforted by what I had discovered. It seemed to fill a void in my life - until I turned 40. A few months after this milestone I woke up one morning and, to my own great surprise, I found I no longer believed in any of my 'New Age' ideas. It's hard to explain, but my belief in the supernatural had vanished overnight. Try as I might, I could not believe in any of my 'isms' any more. This presented a dilemma for me as I had always equated all my beliefs with God. Did this mean that there was no God? I found the whole thing very depressing. For the first time in my life, I had nothing to believe in. My Jazz and Pop career was going well. I was in a relationship with the man who is now my husband. I was successful, but inside I was empty. Looking back, I can see that this was God's hand on my life. In those days, my musical director was a man called Bob Cranham. He was a Christian and more than once he had spoken of what his 'Lord' had done in his life. They were wonderful things, but I could not consider them for myself because I was Jewish. This was the Gentile God blessing His people. In the midst of my turmoil, I called in at his house one day to pick up some music. Now, neither Bob nor his wife knew anything of my inner struggle. Nobody did.

Bob dropped a bombshell that day. He said, *"I'm thinking of giving up the music business."* I asked him why. He said, *"Because I believe God wants me to be a preacher."* I thought to myself, *"Oh dear. He thinks he's hearing from God."* Here was a professional, sane and sensible top-quality musician, composer, song-writer, producer - and he's talking about giving up everything. Nothing I said swayed him. He seemed so calm and sure and so willing to take this drastic step, if, as he believed, God wanted it. I found myself becoming more and more impressed by how real and sincere his faith must be if he could surrender all that for his 'Lord'. I went home and told my boyfriend John how much I envied Bob. I had many opinions, but Bob had real convictions. I wanted what he had! I guess I was 'provoked to jealousy'.

I started to think about this Jesus constantly. I couldn't get Him out of my mind. Finally, I lay awake one night and felt that I had nothing to lose. I whispered, *"Jesus…?"* I half expected to be struck by lightning. *"Are you really there? Are you really the Messiah? If you are, I want to know. Please show me."* (I might as well mention that I had always believed that Jesus existed historically and that he was a Jew. I had never been able to equate the Jewish Jesus with the very un-Jewish artistic depictions of him - blond hair, blue eyes, etc.). Nothing seemed to happen in my room that night, but in the weeks that followed, it seemed that everywhere I went, I was bumping into things and people connected with this Jesus.

While all this was going on, my band and I came back from doing a concert in Germany. When we arrived at the airport and

6

were saying our farewells until the next gig, Bob, my musical director, handed me a book. I was surprised to see that the cover was a picture of a Menorah (a seven-branched lampstand). The title of the book was, 'Betrayed', written by Stan Telchin. The sub-title, in effect, said 'How would you feel as a successful 50-year-old, Jewish businessman if your daughter one day told you she believed in Jesus!' *"How did Bob know I was searching?"* I thought to myself. Of course, he didn't know. Nobody knew.

The book was a total shock. I had heard about the occasional Jewish person believing in Jesus, but I had dismissed them all as weirdos and cranks. But here was a book by a normal, successful Jewish businessman who believed in Jesus and I couldn't ignore it. Outwardly, I showed no emotion. *"OK, I'll read it,"* I said casually. My heart was thumping inside. I couldn't wait to read it. I found out later that Bob had wanted to give me the book for over a year, but the time had never seemed right - until now. How timely that book was. It took me only a couple of hours to finish it. Stan Telchin was a pillar of the Jewish community in Washington D.C., successful in insurance and a member of different Jewish organisations and committees. One day his daughter announced that she had accepted Jesus as her Messiah. After his initial shock and anger wore off, he set out to prove her wrong. He spent months talking to Rabbis, pastors, Jewish believers, Gentile believers, reading the Old and New Testaments, Church history, Jewish history, you name it! After all that, he ended up becoming a believer in Jesus, as did each and every member of his family, one by one.

I learned a great deal from reading this book. Most fascinating of all were the Messianic prophecies he listed. These are prophecies about the Messiah which are found in the Old Testament; the Tenach. I had never heard of them before. Now I learned that in the Law, the Prophets and the Writings there were

7

dozens of specific predictions about a coming Messiah. I had known and loved the 'hit' stories in the Old Testament about Abraham, Isaac, Jacob, Moses, David, Daniel, etc. And I knew that we, the Jewish people, had been promised the Messiah, but I never knew about these many specific, written prophecies. For example, Stan spoke about Isaiah 9:6, where it's written, *"unto us a child is born, unto us a son is given."* I had always thought that verse was in the New Testament as I'd only ever seen it on Christmas cards. But there it was in Isaiah! One of ours! This verse goes on to say that this child would be called, *"wonderful, counsellor, mighty God, everlasting Father, prince of peace."* Mighty God! Is the prophet saying that the Messiah has to be God somehow?

Then Stan quoted Isaiah 7:14, which states that the Messiah would be born of a virgin. I had always thought that talk of a virgin birth was most un-Jewish, but there it was in Isaiah, the Jewish prophet. He also listed Micah 5:2, a verse from one of the so-called 'minor prophets', which speaks of the Messiah being born in Bethlehem, even though he was also from eternity. All of this was amazing enough until I read Psalm 22. It begins with the words *"Eli, Eli, lama azavtani,"* which means, *"My God, My God, why have you forsaken me?"* I had seen enough films about Jesus to know that He cried out these words when He hung on the cross. What I didn't know was that the rest of the Psalm follows on to say, *"they have pierced my hands and my feet…I can count all my bones…they have divided my garments among them and cast lots for my clothing."* It seemed to be a picture of the crucifixion of Jesus. But how could it be? This Psalm was written 1000 years before Jesus and before crucifixion was even invented!

Finally, I came face to face with Isaiah 53, the chapter which speaks at length about one who was to come and take upon himself our sins. *"He was wounded for our trans-gressions, He was bruised for our iniquities, the punishment for our peace was upon Him and with His stripes we are healed. All we, like sheep, have gone astray, each one of us has turned to his own way and the Lord has laid on Him the iniquity of us all."* It seemed to be speaking about Jesus! In fact, all of these prophecies seemed to be painting a picture that I wasn't sure I wanted to see. How come nobody ever showed me these things before? How come all I got was, *"You killed Jesus Christ"*?

I had to find out if these things were really in the Bible. I had to go and buy one. Where do you go to buy a Bible? W.H. Smith of course! I went into their 'religious' section and was confronted with row upon row of Bibles! All shapes and sizes and types. Which one should I buy? There were so many to choose from. Why were there so many? After a long, careful search, I finally selected what seemed to be a straightforward choice - it was called 'The Bible'. I took it home, opened up to the Old Testament, and there they were: prophecies about the Messiah! Dozens of them, speaking of Him coming both as a suffering servant and a victorious king. They all pointed, it seemed to me, to Jesus. Could it really be true? I had come this far - I couldn't go back now. I had to go on. With trepidation, I opened, for the first time in my life, that forbidden book: the New Testament.

I didn't know what to expect. Would it be full of anti-Semitic poison? After all, look at what has been done against the Jews over the centuries in the name of Christ, by those claiming to be Christians. We figured they got it from 'their book'. Imagine my surprise when I opened up the New Testament and was greeted by the most Jewish thing I had seen outside of the Old Testament: the genealogy of Jesus. Not only was I unexpectedly greeted by a list of familiar names, but while reading Stan's book I had learned that the Messiah had to be descended from Abraham, Isaac and Jacob, had to be from the tribe of Judah and of the royal house of David. That was just for starters. All these names were there, and many, many more, in this impeccable lineage of Jesus.

I discovered that the writers of the New Testament were Jewish too. I had always thought that James, Peter and John and co. were Englishmen. To my mind, they couldn't be anything else, with names like that! But I discovered that James was, in fact, Jacob; John was Yochanan; Mary was Miriam; Matthew was Mattityahu; Jesus is Yeshua, which means 'Salvation'! The New Testament is Jewish! Greatly comforted, I began reading about these people, living in the land of Israel, according to the law of Moses. There was a temple and a priesthood - it was a continuation of the Old Testament. I didn't expect it to be like that. And then, there was Jesus. He seemed to rise up out of the pages to me. I was drawn to Him: His words, His compassion, His miracles, His fulfilment of prophecy, his arrest and trial, His crucifixion and resurrection. I finished the Gospel of Matthew and had read halfway through the Gospel of Mark when the thought struck me that I was being too gullible and too easily persuaded. It all seemed too perfect. This Bible, including the Old Testament was, after all, translated by Christians. Maybe they had slanted it towards their way of thinking. I had to be sure. I had to get a 'proper' Bible - a Jewish Bible.

I went to a little Jewish shop in Ilford that sold Judaica in the form of books, cards, religious clothing, etc. I was confronted yet again by wall-to-wall, floor-to-ceiling books. I stood there for what seemed an age, unable to find what I was looking for. The shopkeeper finally came over to me and asked, *"May I help you?"* *"Yes."* I replied, *"I'd like an Old Testament, please." "How old?"* he asked. How embarrassed I felt! I realised my mistake: you don't go into a Jewish shop and ask for an Old Testament. There is no such thing as an Old Testament because there is no such thing as a New Testament. *"You know what I mean!"* I said. Of course he did. He reached up to a top shelf. *"This is what you're looking for,"* he said, handing me a copy of the Tenach, the Holy Scriptures. I got it home and compared it with the Old Testament in my other

Bible from W.H. Smith - it was the same. I was so relieved. I was hoping it would be.

I continued reading the New Testament. By the time I had read all four Gospels, I knew that Jesus was the fulfilment of all the Messianic prophecies. Jesus was and is the Messiah! This was the most wonderful realisation! But what was I to do? This was controversial! I telephoned Bob and said, *"I think I'm on the verge of becoming a believer."* He and his wife asked me over. I had so many questions. One of my main questions was to do with all my old smorgasbord of beliefs: where does God fit in with them? The answer is: He doesn't. Bob showed me from Deuteronomy, right through to Revelation, that all those things are an abomination to God and come under the heading of occult. I learned that I had to repent of and renounce all of those practices.

I told Bob and his wife that I believed that Jesus was the Messiah, the Son of God and God the Son. I believed that He died on the cross, was buried and rose from the dead on the third day. I believed, but I still needed to understand why? They showed me in the Bible, particularly in the letter to the Hebrews, how Jesus was the fulfilment of the sacrificial system, instituted by God when He brought the Israelites out of slavery in Egypt. Whenever God's law was broken, He graciously provided that atonement could be made by the shedding of the blood of an innocent substitute. We have all, Jews and Gentiles, broken God's law and are under His condemnation and are deserving of His punishment. He still requires the shedding of blood. None of our good works or religious rituals can make us right with God.

Thankfully, we don't have to slaughter animals for sacrifice anymore because all of those sacrifices were fulfilled in the once-for-all sacrifice of Jesus on the cross. He was the perfect Lamb of God. The moment He died on the cross, having called out *"It is*

11

finished," the curtain in the Temple that divided the Holy Place from the Holy of Holies was torn in half, from top to bottom. Jesus has paid the penalty for sin and all those who repent and believe in Him can come into the presence of God as cleansed and forgiven worshippers.

They explained that I needed to repent - to turn from my sin back to God. I learned that I was a sinner. We all are. Bob asked me if I would like to respond by praying and asking God to forgive me on the basis of what Jesus has done. Only He can forgive me and only the blood of Jesus can atone for me. I could then commit my life to Him as my Lord and Saviour. This I joyfully did on August 26th, 1987 at 10:30 pm. Even though there were no thunderbolts or flashes of lightning, I knew that my prayer was answered. I can't explain how I knew - I just did. It was all so real and true.

During my search, I had begun to wonder: if I accepted the claims of Jesus and became His follower, would I still be Jewish? Along the way, I had written to Stan Telchin along these lines. He assured me that I would be fulfilling my Jewishness by believing in Jesus, the Messiah of Israel and that I would be coming back to the God of Abraham, Isaac and Jacob. What he said was true. The very reason that God created the Jewish nation was to point to the Messiah. This is the purpose of every Jew. I, along with many others, am fulfilling that very purpose by receiving Jesus as Messiah, Lord and Saviour. Since repenting of my sins and receiving Yeshua - Jesus - I know that I have come out from under the condemnation of the law: eternal separation from God and eternal punishment. We have all, Jew and Gentile, broken the 10 Commandments and are *all* guilty. Only by faith in the perfect sacrifice of Messiah Jesus can we be saved. I urge you to search the Scriptures and find out for yourself.

CHAPTER 2

Betrayed

Stan Telchin
Florida, USA

I am a first generation American whose parents came from Russia in the early 1900's. If you've seen *Fiddler On The Roof* you know what I mean. When I first saw the play I felt that it had been written about my family. My parents were like the couple in the film. They fled Russia to get away from the pogroms and the anti-semitism that was rampant there.

My father, grandfather and uncles all came to New York City in 1904. They came with little more than the clothes on their backs. Even though they did not know English they were soon able to get work to support themselves. Two years later they had saved enough to bring my mother, grandmother and assorted aunts and cousins to the United States. Included in the group was my brother, Charlie, who had been born in Russia after my father had left. Over the next eighteen years five more children were born into our family. On September 14th, 1924, I was born, the youngest and smallest member of the family. I was a premature baby and weighed only 2 pounds 10 ounces at birth.

Until I reached the age of 6, we lived on the lower east side of New York. I began to learn about Jewish ghetto life in America and of the discrimination and prejudices that existed in our country from early childhood. One day, when I was about 5 and in kindergarten I was called a 'Christ killer' for the first time. I didn't know what that expression meant, but I knew that I didn't do it. It was the hatred in the accusation which frightened me more than the words. I remember running home to my mother. We lived at 35 Market Street in Manhattan just a few blocks from the Williamsburg Bridge. I can remember rushing up the stairs to our sixth floor tenement apartment, crying *"Mummy, Mummy."* While I don't remember the exact words my mother used to comfort me, I believe that in calming me she spoke partially in Yiddish and partially in broken English and said, *"Zunnela* [my little son]*, don't cry. Let me tell you something very important that you have to learn...There is 'us', the Jewish people, and there is 'them', the goyim, the Christians. They hate us. And we have to stay away from them. Everything is all right now. Stop crying. No one is going to hurt you. We are in America. And you are safe. Just stay away from them."* As clearly as I can remember the next thing she did was to give me a glass of cold chocolate milk.

Time passed by. We moved to Brooklyn. It was still pretty much a ghetto. 40% of the people in Boro Park at that time were Jewish and 40% were Catholic with the remaining 20% being made up of all others. Our block, 43rd Street, between Fort Hamilton Parkway and 12th Avenue was about 85% Jewish. We lived at 1143, 43rd Street. While not a six-story tenement, it was a four-story walk up. No elevator. We had a four room apartment, a kitchen, a living room, two bedrooms and a bathroom. Although there were six kids in our family, at the time only three of us lived at home. My brother Sam and I shared a bedroom. Mum and Dad shared a bedroom and my sister Dorris slept on a folding bed in the living-dining room. We were crowded, as you can well imagine - bathroom time was sometimes crisis time! But it was 1933 and things were really tough out there in the real world. We were living in the middle of the Depression. Fortunately my father and three brothers were able to find work during those years, and so we managed. But that doesn't mean we escaped the anti-semitism that seemed present everywhere.

I remember one hot summer Sunday morning when I was playing stickball in the school playground at Public School 131 at Fort Hamilton Parkway and 43rd Street. It was almost noon and our game was over. The teams split up and headed for home. As I left School dressed only in shorts and sneakers, I saw this lady heading right for me. She was a large woman dressed completely in black, wearing a black hat and carrying a black purse. The closer she got to me, the more I noticed her piercing look. It frightened me. I remember stopping in my tracks because I didn't know what to do. She kept coming right at me. And as she got up to me she hit me in the chest with her big, black pocket book and said, *"Get out of my way you dirty little Kike!"* I fell to the sidewalk in total amazement. I started to cry. I stood up and ran the hundred yards to our apartment. As I ran up the steps I was again crying *"Mummy, Mummy."* Again my mother had to comfort me. And again my mother reminded me that there is 'us' and there is 'them' - the 'goyim' and the Christians. They hate us. And the best thing we can do is to stay away from them.

I think the first time I ever heard the word 'Messiah' was when I was about seven and America was in the midst of the Depression. I asked my mother for a new bike, something we could definitely not afford. She laughingly told me that I could have it *"Ven de Meshiach kumt"* (when the Messiah comes). I wasn't sure what that meant, but I knew that I would not be getting the bike. The next time I heard the word 'Messiah' was when the news of the Holocaust exploded in our midst. I was about 16 and I heard my mother praying and asking God to send the Messiah to deliver us from the hatred of the world. Though my grandparents were ultra-orthodox, my parents were simply 'conservative' in their observance of Jewish customs and rituals. As I think back over the years of my childhood, I know that we often went to the synagogue, but I can't remember my parents ever really talking with me about God - and we never talked about the Messiah.

I met a girl called Ethel when she became a student at Montauk Junior High School which was located on 16th Avenue between 42nd and 43rd Street in Brooklyn. I was in the eighth grade. She was a brand new seventh grader. While we weren't really friends in school we did have similar interests. We worked on the newspaper together. We were also in a band. I played the trumpet and she played a flute.

Later, we went to different high schools and didn't see much of each other during those later school years. Then came the army. In December 1944, just before I went overseas in World War II, I was home on furlough and went to visit a lady called Helen, a good friend of mine whose husband was in the service too. I had only been there for about an hour when the doorbell rang. It was Ethel. She had also come to visit Helen. Later, as we were leaving Helen's apartment I asked her if I could walk her home. We walked and walked, and talked and talked. Then as we were parting, Ethel asked me if I wanted her to write to me. *"What a question,"* I replied. *"Good! And I'll send you some packages."* Fifteen months later, when the war was over and I was finally discharged, I went to Ethel's house to thank her for her letters and packages. She looked wonderful to me! We had our first date the very next day and two years later, on May 26th, 1948 we were married.

Ethel was a very special lady and we had an exceptionally happy marriage over the years (she passed away in 2000). We were blessed with two beautiful daughters, Judy and Ann. Then there were the material things. Twenty six years into our marriage we had a very large home complete with swimming pool, four BMW's and a full-time housekeeper. I was a Chartered Life Underwriter, a member of the Million Dollar Round Table and was very successful financially. Then, just months later, my world was turned upside down. Judy, my 21 year old daughter, who was then a student at Boston University, phoned me at 10.30pm one

16

Sunday evening. My wife was in the shower. My other daughter, Ann, 17, was in her room doing homework.

"Hi, Dad. It's Judy. Can you talk?"
"Sure I can talk, Jude. Everything OK?"
"I'm fine, Dad. But what I have to say is very important."

There was a strange edge to Judy's voice. Alarm bells started ringing in my head. Something is wrong.

"What is it Judy? What's happened?"
"Now don't be alarmed, Dad. I'm okay. It's just that I've been wanting to talk to you all day. Can Mum get on the other phone?"
"Mum's taking a shower."
"Well, okay. You can tell her later."
"I'm listening, Jude."
"Dad, I've written you a very long letter. I've spent days on it. I finished it this morning and have been reading and rereading it all day. But I can't post it to you. I don't want it to hurt you. This is the hardest thing I've ever tried to do. I want to read the letter to you now. May I, Dad?"

I fought off a series of negative thoughts which raced through my mind: she was pregnant...she had run off and got married...she had been expelled from University. But since Judy was such a wonderful daughter - so mature and sensible - none of these thoughts made any sense. I forced myself to remain calm.

"Jude, wait a minute before you start reading. Let me get paper and pencil so that I can make notes."

When I returned to the phone my daughter hesitated and then once again apologised for what she was about to tell me. She was now speaking quite rapidly and I could feel my own throat tighten in response to her anxiety.

17

"Dear Mum and Dad" she began. *"It's hard for me to write this letter because I love you and Ann so much. I never knew a family could be as close as we are..."*

Numbly I listened to Judy describe in detail all that she loved about our family. Then as she went on to describe a recent period of loneliness my hand tightened on the phone. But she had solved the loneliness by taking on a job at an emergency hot line where she was able to help 'people in need' through the telephone. Then she began to tell me about Richard. Richard was a 'Bible believer' she said. He worked on the hot line too. They had become friends. Richard would talk to Judy about the Bible at length and when Judy explained that she had never read the Bible, he bought her one. Over the months he would suggest passages she should read.

"I had long talks with Richard, Dad, and from what I learned in those talks and read in the Bible and a whole lot of other things too, well..."

I held my breath as she paused for composure.

"Well, I've become a believer too."

There was a long moment of silence.

"What does that mean Judy?"

"It means that I believe in God. I believe that the Bible is the word of God and [long pause] *I believe that Jesus is the Messiah."*

I was speechless. I was outraged. I felt betrayed. How could a child of mine join the enemy? As the 45 minute conversation continued, I realized I had two options: I could disown her immediately for this terrible act or I could love her through it. I decided on the second option.

I drew the conversation to a conclusion. After I put the phone down I felt absolutely drained. Two weeks later Judy came home for her spring vacation. We talked and talked and talked. I don't remember much of what Judy said, but I remember that I kept saying *"But Judy, you are Jewish! You can't believe in Jesus! You can't be Jewish and believe in Jesus!"* To which she would reply, *"Daddy, that isn't true. Some Jews have always believed in Jesus!"*

Just before she left to return to school, Judy challenged me to do something I had never done. *"Daddy, you are an educated man. You have all sorts of degrees. Read the Bible for yourself and make up your own mind. It is either true or it is false. And if you read it carefully and ask God to reveal the truth to you, He will."* I understood what Judy wanted to accomplish by that challenge, but I saw it as a way to disprove what she believed. Immediately I decided to read the Bible. I planned to gather enough information to prove that Jesus is *not* the Messiah. By doing so, I would win her back!

After dinner, the very next night, I picked up the New Testament for the very first time. As I set out to read the book of Matthew, I was prepared for a book of hate aimed at the Jewish people. What else could it be? *"The Christians get their hate for us either from their mother's milk or from this book,"* I thought. But I didn't find it to be a book of hate. It was a book written by a Jew, for other Jews, about the God of Abraham, Isaac and Jacob and the Messiah He sent to His people.

The next night I read the book of Mark. Wednesday was Luke. On Thursday and Friday I read John. My notepad was filling up with lots and lots of questions. On Saturday morning I began to read the Acts of the Apostles. All went well until I came to the tenth chapter of this book. There I read about Peter reluctantly going to the house of a Gentile called Cornelius, a Roman Centurion. Peter didn't want to be there. He didn't want to be with this Gentile. But Cornelius explained that he had had a vision in which he was told that Peter would tell him about God. With that prompting, Peter began to tell Cornelius about the God of Abraham, Isaac and Jacob and about Jesus, the Messiah. While he was speaking something totally unexpected happened: the Holy Spirit fell upon Cornelius and on all the Gentiles in his home. Peter and the Jewish believers who were with him were astonished. How could this be? How could the Spirit fall upon Gentiles? That wasn't supposed to happen! The Spirit of God had been given to the Jews! He had not come to the Gentiles!

In the very next chapter of The Acts, I read about how Peter was in Jerusalem at a meeting of the Jerusalem Council. The Jewish believers at that meeting were very upset with Peter because he had broken bread with a Gentile and had shared the Messiah with him and his family. Naturally, Peter explained what had happened and how the Holy Spirit had fallen on the Gentiles in Cornelius' house. At this report, the Council decided that God is not a 'respector of persons' (partial or biased) and that Jesus the Messiah must be for Gentiles as well as for Jews! As I read these things, I was stunned. How could this be? How was it possible that two thousand years ago the Messiah was only for the Jews and not for the Gentiles - and now He is only for the Gentiles and not for Jews? What had happened over the years?

As I began my study, I remember writing down a series of vital questions. Each question led to the next. Do I really believe in God? Do I believe that the Tenach is God's word to us or is it only a human account of the Jewish people? Does the Tenach contain prophecies about a Messiah Who is to come? Has anyone ever lived who fulfilled these prophecies? Did Jesus fulfill them? I knew that if I received a 'no' answer to any of these questions, my study would be over. But if each question produced a 'yes' I would be in serious trouble, because the last thing in the world that I

20

wanted to believe was that Jesus is the Jewish Messiah.

The next days, weeks and months were filled with study. After a few days, I took a leave of absence from my business so that I could have more time for study. I read the entire New Covenant and a good portion of the Tenach. I went to the Library and obtained books about the Jewish religion and Jewish history. I talked to rabbis. I studied the Messianic prophecies in the Tenach. I didn't know how many prophecies the Tenach contained, but I came up with a list of over 40 of them. And it staggered me to realise that Jesus fulfilled each and every one of them! Of particular significance to me in my study of Scripture was Jeremiah 31:31-34, where God promised to make a New Covenant with the Jewish people!

How could I have been fifty years old and not known of this promise? And then there was Proverbs 30:4 which spoke of God's Son; and the 22nd Psalm which revealed Jesus hanging on a tree; and Isaiah chapter 53 which explained that our sins were placed upon Him and that He was punished instead of us; and Daniel 9 which prophesied that Jerusalem would be destroyed along with the Temple by the prince who would come *after* the Messiah had been killed! By now I knew when that had taken place. It was in the year 70 CE! I was stunned by this realization. I remember writing *"Either the Messiah came and died before the year 70 or the Bible is merely the story of the Jewish people and not the word of God!"* The more I thought about the Scriptures, the more convinced I became that Jesus really is the Jewish Messiah. And that is something I did not want to even acknowledge, much less believe!

Months into my study, I decided to attend a meeting of 'Messianic Jews', Jews who believe that Jesus is the Messiah. At this meeting I met a woman named Lillian. When she found out that I was not yet a believer in Jesus, she offered me her Bible and asked me to read Exodus 20:2-3 aloud to her. I read: "*I am the LORD your God, who has brought you out of the land of Egypt, out of the house of bondage. You shall have no other gods before me.*"

When I finished reading, Lillian asked me to close the Bible and then said: "Tell me Stan, who is your God? Is He the God of our Fathers, the God of Abraham, Isaac and Jacob or are you worshipping false gods like your business, your home, your wife, your children? What do you spend your time thinking about? Whom do you worship?" I was struck by Lillian's questions and realised that I spent a good part of my time thinking and even worshipping these things. But I almost never thought about God or considered worshipping Him. Lillian's questions did their work and the pressure within me kept building. I knew that in my heart I believed that Jesus is the Messiah, but I was afraid to confess this with my mouth. I was afraid of the consequences such a decision would have on my life, on the life of my family and on my business. I remember arguing with myself. I remember raising the objections of the Crusades and the Inquisition and the Pogroms and the Holocaust. As if to answer each argument I would raise, on the inside of me I would hear: "*Yes, but it's true! Jesus is the Messiah!*" The next day July 3, 1975 at 7:15 in the morning, the pressure within finally found it's release. It burst forth from my lips. Jesus is our Messiah! He is my Messiah! I do receive Him as the Lord of my life! When I told my wife, expecting a hostile reaction, I found out that she had already repented and accepted the Lord Jesus as her Messiah and Saviour and had just been waiting for me to come to the same realisation! Now our whole family is united again.

I invite my readers to do exactly what I did. With an open mind search the scriptures - specifically the Messianic prophecies - and be honest with your findings. You have nothing to fear. Indeed, you will know the truth and the truth will set you free.

CHAPTER 3

Holocaust

Rabbi Sam Stern
Warsaw, Poland.

I was born at a time when the whole world lay in turmoil - during the 1914-18 World War. I grew up in a strict orthodox Jewish home. Although my parents were poor at that time, they made sacrifices and sent my three brothers and me to a private orthodox school. My father was a devout rabbi who prayed three times a day at the synagogue. His overiding desire in life was to make rabbis of us boys.

By the age of seven I was able to read Hebrew. At nine I was introduced to the five books of Moses, the Bible commentator Rashi and also to the ancient Jewish books of jurisprudence called the Talmud. By the time I reached my eleventh birthday, the Talmud had eclipsed all the other books and became my main textbook from then on. I was under my father's jurisdiction until 13, at which age I was free from his supervision. I was taken to a synagogue where my father thanked God that he was no longer responsible for my sins!

My family lived in a little town in Congress, near Warsaw, Poland. 500 Jewish and 800 Polish families lived there, divided by culture, language and religion. The Jews were not granted the privilege of working for the municipal and federal government, nor in factories and agriculture. We were two peoples living in one territory, under the same Polish sky, eating the same Polish bread and breathing the same Polish air - yet we were as strange to each other as the East is from the West. Growing up I inevitably came into contact with Gentiles. Sometimes they threw stones at me and shouted *"Jew, Jew."* My mother told me the reason:

"They are Christians and Christians are Jew-haters. But when our Messiah comes, we shall be the head and not the tail. Then we will go back to Palestine and no one will persecute us any more."

"But when will the Messiah come?" I asked.

"We don't know the exact time, but He will come some day. Then our sufferings at the hands of the Christians will come to an end."

The hope of the coming Messiah accompanied me all my life. It gave me power to endure suffering and humiliation from my Gentile neighbours. After my Bar Mitzvah I was sent to a higher rabbinical school. For 9 years I studied the sixty books of the Talmud as I trained to become a Rabbi. By the age of 22 I was considered a 'lamdan' which means a man who is learned in the Talmud.

In September 1939, World War II broke out. I had just received my rabbinical diploma called 'Smicha' that past summer. I had planned to marry and become a religious leader of Israel - to make good use of my acquired knowledge to lead my fellow-Jews in the ways of the Talmudic, rabbinic traditions. An alternative plan was to leave Poland, perhaps to emigrate to a country in Latin America where there was a great need for rabbis. The war destroyed all my plans. My very life was in danger, as was that of all European Jewry. On September 4, the German soldiers came into our town. Life was never to be the same again - it soon became unbearable for Polish Jews. Every Jew was condemned to

24

die. If all the skies were parchment, all men writers, and all trees pens, even then it would not be possible to adequately describe what the Nazis did to the Jews in Poland and the rest of Europe. Within 6 years, 6 million Jews, among them 1 million children, were murdered. One third of the world's Jewish population was annihilated. Yes, here and there a conscientious Polish family rescued a Jew, hiding him and feeding him, but the number of these good people was tragically small.

Finally, in May 1945, the War was over. I was in a Concentration Camp but I had survived. I had high hopes of seeing my relatives again. I put advertisements in newspapers. I went to different institutions. To my great sorrow I learned that all my loved ones had perished. I came to realize the bitter fact that I was alone in the world without a friend - belonging to no one and no one belonging to me. I couldn't believe it; I would never see my parents, my sister, my brothers or my uncles and aunts again. I started to look for a friend in this strange new world, but not surprisingly none could satisfy my longing for a true mother's heart or a father's love. I was disappointed and desperate. I lifted my eyes up to heaven and asked the question - why? Why was one third of the nation of God put to death by the Nazis? Where was God when little innocent Jewish children cried for help and the Nazi murderers raised their brutal hands to kill them? Why was God silent in these terrible times for His chosen people?

Since I had no one in Poland, I decided to go to America. I thought that perhaps in a new land I would forget the dreadful past and start a new life. In order to go to America I had to go first to Germany. In April 1946 I came to a Jewish D.P. Camp near the Austrian border of Germany. I registered there as a rabbi and started to work as such in the D.P. Camp. I also edited the D.P. newspaper. Finally, in 1952 I came to Rhode Island, U.S.A., where I worked as an assistant rabbi. Although I worked in the capacity of a Talmudic teacher in the synagogue, there remained a great conflict in my heart. Why had God allowed 6 million Jews to die? This question simply would not go away.

I taught things I was no longer sure were true. *"If we Jews want to exist and to overcome our enemies we have to keep the Sabbath day holy,"* I used to say. But in my heart I knew that most of Hitler's victims had kept the Sabbath-day holy, yet it had not protected them. I did not have any proof or assurance any more. I lost my belief in the Talmudic legends, laws, and arguments pro and con. I was looking for the truth, but could not find it.

Each holiday we went to the synagogue and prayed to God, confessing our sins, and asking for forgiveness. We said, *"Because of our sins we were driven from our land."* Confession of sins was a very important part of our prayers. The Jewish prayer-book cites different kinds of sins which a Jew must confess in his daily prayers. The most solemn day of prayer is Yom Kippur, one evening of which every Jew over 13 years of age must recite 45 confessions called 'Al Chets'. After the confession, the 'Slach Lanu' (forgive us) is chanted by the congregation.

When I prayed these prayers I felt unhappy and dissatisfied because I knew that according to the Bible, confession alone does not forgive sin. I knew that in order for sin to be forgiven, a sacrifice called 'korban' must be offered. Leviticus deals with the korban many times (see Lev 5:17-19). I was not sure that the Yom Kippur prayers had any significance in the sight of God, because I knew that right after the confessions and prayers we went back to the same old pattern of a life of sin. It seemed to me that as we were confessing our sins in the synagogue, we were mocking God. We spoke with our lips about repentance but didn't really mean it.

I felt very unhappy with my spiritual state of mind. I lost

faith in mankind and in the rabbinical legends and teachings. I felt miserable knowing that I, as a rabbi, was teaching the people things that I did not believe. I knew that the Talmudic teachings, sayings, scholastic debates, hair-splitting comments about obsolete damages, laws, rules and regulations regarding Sabbath, Holy Days, clothing and washings, were really of very little significance to us. I realized that we needed a really solid spiritual truth by which to live as Jews. But what was the truth? I did not know. I looked on my people as sheep without a shepherd. I saw that 2,000 years of Talmudic, chasidic, cabbalistic and worldly teachings could not save one Jew from destruction.

One spring evening I walked somewhere in Rhode Island. I looked aimlessly here and there just breathing the fresh spring air. While I strolled, I noticed some young people standing near a shop handing out leaflets. They caught my attention so I took what they were offering. As I could not read English I decided to go into the store to find out what kind of 'sale' they were having. When I went inside I was surprised to see that there was nothing 'on sale'. To my astonishment I noticed every one sitting with eyes closed and heads bowed. *"What is going on here?"* I thought to myself. I waited a while till everybody had finished. A boy came and talked to me, but I did not understand him. I told him that I spoke only German and Yiddish. Through the use of sign language I made a date to come back the next Wednesday. It was arranged that a German-speaking person would come and explain to me what the organization was.

The next Wednesday the German gentleman was waiting for me. He shook my hand warmly and said to me in German,

"This is a mission to the Jews."

"What is a mission?" I asked.

"The Lord sent us to the Jews to let them know that God loves them and wants them to be saved."

"What do you mean saved? How can you speak about love after the cataclysm that came over the European Jew?" I asked.

He smiled and said, *"I know how you feel, but real Christians, followers of Christ, love the Jews, and all those who harm them are not true Christians."*

I retorted, *"Weren't all those who carried crosses and had pictures of saints in their homes - yet organised pogroms against the Jews of Europe - weren't they Christians? Weren't the churches in Poland and Ukraine the main source of anti-Semitism? Didn't the priests incite their people against the Jews?"*

He looked at me and said, *"The Lord teaches us to love our enemies, to show love to those who hate us. All those who do not obey the teachings of the Lord are not His followers."*

Then he gave me a Yiddish New Testament and said, *"Read it and you will find the true teaching of Christ."*

In the next few nights I had much to read. Every line, each page, was a revelation to me. Beginning with the Book of Matthew, I was surprised to read that Jesus is of the lineage of Abraham and David. I also noticed that on nearly every page it says *"As it is written"*, meaning 'written in the Jewish Bible'. For example, in the first chapter I read that the Messiah will be born of a virgin as it is written in Isaiah, *"Behold a virgin shall be with child and shall bring forth a son and you shall call his name Immanuel"* (Isaiah 7:14).

In the 2nd chapter of Matthew I read that the Messiah was

to be born in Bethlehem, as it is written: *"And you Bethlehem in the land of Judah are not the least among the princes of Judah, for out of you shall come forth a governor that shall rule my people Israel"* (Micah 5:2). Also I saw that He would visit and return out of Egypt, for it is written: *"Out of Egypt have I called my son"* (Hosea 11:1). It seemed there were constant references to the Old Testament throughout the gospel according to Matthew. It became clear to me that this book called the New Testament is actually the fulfilment of the Old Testament. Right there and then I became a Bible-believing Jew. I thanked God for leading me to that little Mission and decided to dedicate my life to the Messiah.

It was a few weeks before Passover. The missionary in Rhode Island gave me the address of a Jewish believer in Jesus who lived in New York. I had never met such a person before! As soon as I contacted him, he invited me to his home. He greeted me with, *"Shalom Aleichem"*. We read toge-ther from the New Testament in Yiddish. After a while he told me he had written a poem called 'The Sufferer' and started to read it. Then he asked me, *"Who is the subject of this poem? Who suffered for our sins? By whose stripes are we healed?"*

I answered, *"It probably refers to Jesus Christ."*

Then he said, *"I just copied out and read to you the 53rd chapter of Isaiah. He was the one who wrote about the Messiah."*

Imagine my surprise! What he had pretended was a poem was actually a chapter from the Jewish Bible. I did not know about Isaiah 53. That day I showed the same 'poem' to a friend in New York. He did not know it was a chapter from Isaiah either. The only conclusion I could reach was that the main reason so many Rabbis and other Jews don't know the Messiah, the Saviour of the Old and New Testament, is that they don't know the Bible.

The same evening I went back to the New York missionary and told him that I believe in the Bible and in the Lord Jesus. We knelt together and prayed for the forgiveness of sin and for salvation. As a repentant sinner I accepted the Lord Jesus as my personal Saviour. What a change came over me - I was so happy! I felt a peace, joy and happiness that I had never known before. I was a new person. When I came home I took the Bible and read the 53rd chapter of Isaiah over and over again. As I read I wondered why I had not heard of Isaiah 53 before. Why didn't the Rabbis tell me about this chapter? It was obvious to me that we Jews could not be considered Bible-believers if we deny Isaiah 53. As I read more, it became clear to me that Isaiah's prophecy in chapter 53 expresses God's glorious plan of forgiveness, reconciliation with God and salvation clearer than perhaps any other passage of scripture.

I went to Los Angeles and started my American education. After finishing 8 grades I graduated from high school. Later I went to Los Angeles City College, and finally to Biola College, where I received a B.A. degree. I was baptized and eventually became a preacher of the Gospel. I had come a long way. With the Lord Jesus as my Messiah it felt like the difference between darkness and light. Ever since that day it has been my one desire that others of my fellow-Jews should also come to know the one spoken of in Isaiah 53.

CHAPTER 4

The Forbidden Book

Rabbi Chil Slotowski
Tel-Aviv, Israel

As a descendant of a line of orthodox Jewish Rabbis I received a strict rabbinical education. I thank God for a mind which enabled me at the age of 17 years to obtain the highest diplomas of two Rabbinical Seminaries. These distinctions, however, did not satisfy me and I continued earnestly to study the Talmud, the Shulchan Aruch and other rabbinical works. When I was 20 years old I knew much of the Talmud and other commentaries on the Old Testament by heart. On account of my thorough knowledge of those books many Rabbis used to consult me concerning Kashrut questions, and in spite of my youth they accepted my decisions as correct.

At the age of 25 I became Rabbi at Dubno in Poland. I was strictly orthodox and rejected every opinion that did not comply with the letter of Talmudic traditions. Two years later I had a call to Lodz, a large town in Poland. There I held not only the position of a Rabbi, but became also a Professor at the Rabbinical Seminary. In my lectures I admonished the students to abhor Christianity. I believed all the terrible stories about Jesus contained in the Talmud. However, through God's gracious providence, I became acquainted at that time with a well-educated Missionary. He knew the Talmud and began to converse with me. What he told me was extremely interesting - so much so that I paid him frequent visits. Very soon my relatives got to know about this and became very disturbed. They discussed the matter and then decided to write, without my knowledge, to the Chief Rabbi of Palestine, T. Cook. Rabbi Cook knew my name through our Kashrut correspondence. He was told of *"the great danger which threatened my soul,"* because of my association with a Christian Missionary. They implored him to have pity on my soul and to save me from this disastrous situation by extending to me a call to Palestine and obtaining for me a permit to enter that country. They were convinced that in this way I would be quickly delivered from the bad influence of this Missionary. During all that time I had not the slightest idea of what was going on.

A few weeks later I received a letter from the Chief Rabbi of Palestine. He mentioned quite casually that he could obtain a permit for me to enter Palestine should I wish to come there. I was delighted at the prospect of going to the land of my forefathers and accepted his suggestion joyfully. A month later I left for Palestine. Shortly after my arrival, the Chief Rabbi appointed me as Secretary to the Chief Rabbinate of Jerusalem. Moreover he continually showed me his special favour and liked to have me near him. His interest in me became so obvious that I began to wonder what might be the reason.

One day I frankly asked him about the matter. He told me of the correspondence with my relatives and tried to convince me of the falseness of the Missionary's teachings. Here I must confess that the Missionary's words had penetrated only my mind - not my heart. Sometimes the truth takes many years to proceed from the head into the heart and so it was in my case. In consequence of the Chief Rabbi's talks I began to think that he might be right. Gradually the Missionary's conversations faded from my mind.

After the death of Rabbi Cook I accepted a call as Talmud

teacher at the Rabbinical Seminary of Tel Aviv where I taught for two years. One day I travelled in the company of several members of my Committee by train from Haifa to Jerusalem. Opposite me in our compartment there sat a young man reading a little book. On the cover I could see very clearly the words 'New Testament' in Hebrew. At once I knew that he was a Jewish Christian, Jewish because he read Hebrew and Christian because he read the New Testament. In the presence of the members of my Committee I felt obliged to protest to the young man and to reproach him for reading such a strictly forbidden book as the New Testament. I criticized him severely and made known to him my position as a Rabbi. To my surprise the young man did not get annoyed but smiled at me and said: *"Perhaps you will show me what you find offensive in the book and I will try to explain it."*

What he said took my mind back to the time when I had superficially read a little of the New Testament. I knew of nothing repugnant in the book. What could I say? What annoyed me most at that moment was the presence of my fellow-travellers. I had to give the young man a suitable reply so as not to lose my friends' respect. I replied somewhat lamely: *"How can I show you wrong statements in a book which we are forbidden to read?"* He answered: *"How can you criticize and judge something of which you have no knowledge? First read the book, please, and then you will see that there is nothing whatsoever in it that could be criticized."* I remained silent.

Suddenly my discussions with the Missionary came back to me. Why had I run away from his instructions? Like lightning, these thoughts moved within my soul. Obviously the young man noticed the confused expression in my eyes. While my companions were distracted and looking the other way he whispered to me: *"I see you are interested in these things. May I give you this New Testament? Please take it; I have another one at home."* Quickly I took the little book and put it in my pocket.

That same evening I began reading the New Testament in my room at Jerusalem. Before opening it, however, I had prayed: *"Open mine eyes, that I may behold wondrous things out of your law"* (Psalm 119:18). In His grace the Lord heard my prayer and showed me things which I had never seen before. While reading I felt the creation of a clean heart and of a right spirit within me (Psalm 51:10) and there was new light (Psalm 119:105). Like a thirsty man drinks greedily when he has found a spring of fresh, cool water, so I drank in page after page of the New Testament. In one long session I read all of Matthew, Mark and Luke - until I noticed the clock said 3 a.m.!

With every page there grew and deepened the conviction that Jesus Christ is the Messiah prophesied to us Jews. Slowly but surely my burdened heart, soul and spirit became free and joyful. This was an entirely new and strange feeling for which I could find no name at the time. I could not have described it; yet, it was so real. Certain chapters of the Holy Scriptures attracted me in a special way and I can recollect still many of them. The Sermon on the Mount opened up before me a new world, a world full of beauty and glory. The proclaimer of such a lovely world cannot be evil whatever the Talmud says.

I was deeply impressed also by Luke 23:34, *"Then said Jesus, Father, forgive them; for they know not what they do."* Compare this utterance with that of Jeremiah when he was oppressed. Jeremiah cursed his persecutors. Jesus, on the other hand, even when nailed to the cross, had nothing but forgiveness, mercy, sympathy and prayer for His persecutors. What a difference! How much greater He must be than the prophets! My soul was so touched by what I had read that, although it was three o'clock in the morning, for the first time in my life I knelt down and prayed. Jews pray standing and not kneeling. I cannot say for how long I prayed but I know that never before had I prayed with such fervour and purpose. I

34

wept and implored God for light. I beseeched Him to show me the truth: what was right and what was wrong, the Talmud or the New Testament. And for the first time I prayed in the name of Jesus!

After that prayer there came into my heart such peace and joy as I had never experienced before, not even on the Day of Atonement, although on that day I always fasted and prayed fervently. Never before did I have such certainty of reconciliation with God as I felt then and have known ever since. I knew and had no doubt whatever that the Lord Jesus is the long-prophesied Messiah of the Jews and the Saviour of the world, and I came to see in Him my personal Redeemer. Then I went to bed; but after this vivid experience I was unable to sleep. Soon I felt a voice saying to me: *"Never again wander away from Me! I will use you for the glory of My name and as a witness to My saving grace."* I immediately answered: *"Lord, here am I."* From then onward my life no longer belonged to me but to Him and so it is still. For in that solemn moment I turned from my sin and surrendered myself completely and unreservedly to Him. Even that, I felt, was little enough a repayment for all He had done for me when He saved my soul from eternal damnation.

At first I was no more than a secret believer. In my inward being I knew that the Lord Jesus Christ was the Messiah of Israel but I continued nevertheless to fulfil my tasks and duties as Rabbi. I lived like this for two months. But oh! how depressed and miserable my soul was. At last I realized that I could no longer lead a double life. I had to confess Christ publicly - whatever the consequences might be. The same day I resigned as a Rabbi. The Committee Members were dismayed. They earnestly asked me not to leave and offered me a higher stipend. It was then that I witnessed to them frankly of Jesus, telling them that he is the long-expected Messiah and my personal Redeemer. Immediately persecution followed but I was not intimidated in any way. I had expected persecution. I was stoned on the street and had to stay in bed for some time while the doctor came twice a day to attend to and bandage my wounds. When my fellow-Jews saw that persecution did not move me they tried another plan: a prominent Jewish man offered to adopt me as his son and heir provided I would renounce Christianity. I told him: *"If you can give me peace for my soul, procure me the presence of God and pardon for my sins, I will return to Judaism."* He answered: *"That I cannot do for I do not possess myself what you are asking."* He never approached me again.

Later, when I was in such danger that I did not know where to turn, I met an American Missionary in a Bible shop. He talked to me in Hebrew and when he heard that I had come to Christ and was in danger of my life, he advised me to leave immediately for Beirut in Syria and gave me a letter of introduction to an evangelical church there. I went and two months later was baptized. Eventually, after becoming more experienced in the scriptures, I returned to the land of my forefathers in order to work among my own people witnessing to them of Jesus Christ.

My method of work was two fold. First I showed from passages in the Old Testament that the Lord Jesus is the true and long-predicted Messiah of Israel. I have found more than 200 passages which prove this fact beyond any doubt. Secondly I showed the superiority of the New Testament teachings to those of the Talmud. God's blessing rested on this method, and a number of my brethren to whom I have witnessed have come to believe in the Lord Jesus Christ as their Redeemer.

CHAPTER 5

My Search

Robert B. Greenberg M.D.
Louisville, KY, U.S.A.

I was born in Brooklyn, N.Y., in 1941, into an orthodox Jewish family. My heritage is a long line of Russian Rabbis and cantors on my mother's side, and Levites on my father's side. I attended Talmud-Torah for five years and learned Hebrew, Chumash (the five books of Moses) and the teachings of Rabbinnic Judaism, with much emphasis on tradition and liturgy. Except perhaps for occasional references, we did not study the Talmud too much. At my Barmitzvah at the age of 13, I was given the privilege of conducting the entire service with a choir and chanting my Haftorah (a portion of the prophets, in my case Ezekiel 22) directly from the scroll without the vowels. How proud my relatives and Rabbi were that day! I continued my studies in orthodox customs and observances for several years into my teens.

Unfortunately however, with high school and college, I lost a good deal of interest in Judaism, although I continued to be aware of my rich Jewish heritage and never ceased to believe in God and to pray. I decided to become a Doctor and, with much encouragement and help from my parents, was accepted into medical school, where I spent four difficult years of study. This was in addition to the five years of undergraduate study which preceded my medical curriculum. It was during this time that I

37

began to feel something was missing in my life and began searching for the meaning of life.

I searched everywhere and tried out various philosophies, cults, religions and New Age ideas. Although initially I would be enthusiastic and was frequently deceived into believing I had at last found the best answer to life's deep problems and questions, none ultimately satisfied me. There was always a certain amount of truth in each new idea, but they all came to a dead end.

While in medical school I became interested in psychiatry, partly as a result of my desire to know more about myself and what makes other people tick. Amazingly, it was through psychiatry that I found something, or should I say *someone*, real. A psychiatrist had written a book about Jesus Christ, which presented Him as a wonderful person. This presentation shocked me as I had never up to that time known anything significant about the life of Christ. This book constantly referred to another book which I had never read and was actually afraid of. It was called the New Testament.

I obtained my first ever copy at 23 years of age. I took it out and opened it. I saw strange book titles: 'Acts', 'Romans', 'Corinthians'. I did not know the meaning of these words, so I turned back to a section with people's names; Matthew, Mark, Luke and John (Hebrew, Yochanan). I correctly assumed that these men had written accounts of the life of the Messiah. I began reading John and the first important thing I noticed was that this book was not just a series of stories about a great prophet, but there was also a power behind the words which made me feel different. I discovered later that the New Testament writers were all Jews and that Jesus was a Jew. The New Testament (Covenant) wonderfully fulfills the promises of the Old Testament (Tenach) and is at once its continuation and completion. After three more years of occasional reading, combined with some important experiences, it gradually dawned on me that Yeshua (Jesus) was more than just a wonderful person - He was the Jewish Messiah, the unique Son of God. He died as the Passover lamb to make atonement for Jew and Gentile alike.

Judaism taught me that there were three levels of sacrifice for sin in Israel: *individual sacrifices*, such as Abraham offered; *family sacrifices* such as the Passover in Egypt, and later *national sacrifices* such as was offered by the high priest on Yom Kippur (Day of Atonement). But where is the next logical sacrifice - a *universal* one? I found this in the New Covenant sacrifice of the Messiah Himself - the Lord Jesus Christ. In 1967 I knelt in repentance and accepted Him as my personal Lord and Saviour - it was then that I experienced the love and presence of God in my life.

I continued with five more years of additional surgical, medical, neurological and psychiatric training. In 1972 I began a two year service commitment as an army medical officer specialising on psychiatry. The Vietnam War was in progress and through a series of interesting circumstances, I was promoted to major and made chief of the department of neuro-psychiatry in an army hospital in the USA. I befriended the chaplain there and told him of my faith in Jesus as my Messiah who had died for my sins and risen again from the dead. We met together regularly for fellowship and I began to grow in my faith in Christ. In 1974, with the Vietnam War over, I 'accidentally' met a preacher who told me that there were many more Jews who believed Jesus was the Messiah. Up to then I had thought I was the only one in the world! What a joy to meet many of my fellow-Jewish brothers and sisters who share my faith in Christ!

There are many deeply ingrained misconceptions about Yeshua among the Jewish people, which have been complicated by Satan's persecutions of Jews in the name of Jesus. I discovered that more *Gentile* believers in Christ, real Christians that is, were killed during the Spanish Inquisition than Jews! The question in many Jewish minds is *"How can I follow Christ and remain a Jew?"* However, the real question should be how can I, a Jew, reject my Jewish Saviour who became like His Jewish brethren and died for them? What kind of love must He have had for us to provide our needed kapporah (atonement) for sin and become our substitute?

CHAPTER 6

For the Reader

The 13 principles of Judaism accepted by Orthodox Jews contain the words:

> *"I believe with perfect faith in the coming of the Messiah, and, though He tarry, I wait daily for His coming"* (Article 12, Authorized Daily Prayer Book, p. 95).

But how would you recognise the Messiah? Traditional biblical Judaism says the Messiah will do three things:

1) Secure the land for Israel
2) Bring peace to Israel and the world
3) Rebuild the temple on its historical site.

However, with so-many pseudo Jewish Messiahs like Bar Kochba (135AD), David Alroy (1147), Abraham Abulafia (1284), Solomon Molko (1530), Shabbetai Zvi (1665) and Jacob Frank (1726-1791), none of whom met the Messianic qualifications, is it any wonder that the Messianic hope is being reinterpreted today? Many in Judaism today look, not for a personal Messiah, but for a 'Messianic age' of peace in the world.

Meeting a stranger at an airport can be tricky. You look into a sea of faces and wonder how you will know who your contact is. What you need is a photo or at least a description of the person - then you can be certain to find them. The Jewish scriptures actually provide a photo-fit of the Messiah which is *so detailed* that only one person in history could ever fit it. Thus no truly open-minded person could fail to recognise Him after doing their own research. Here are eight examples of these amazing photo-fit prophecies which were all written down by Jewish prophets and Kings hundreds of years before Jesus was born. The Messiah was prophesied in the following terms:

1. In chapter 7 verse 14 of his prophecy, Isaiah says that the Messiah will be born of a virgin. This was fulfilled by Jesus, the son of David, in Matthew 1:23.

2. Micah, in chapter 5:2, says that the Messiah will be born in Bethlehem. This was fulfilled in Jesus' birth in Matthew 2:1.

3. Daniel the prophet states, in chapter 9 verse 26 of his prophecy, that the Messiah will appear on the scene *before* the destruction of the second temple (which happened in AD 70). This time frame perfectly fits the life of Jesus.

4. In the 16th verse of the 22nd Psalm, King David speaks of the fact that the Messiah's hands and feet will be pierced. This was before crucifixion was known among the Jewish nation. However it came true - Jesus was crucified, despite being pronounced innocent three times by Pilate the Roman judge (Luke 23:33).

5. The prophet Zechariah states that the Messiah would be sold for 30 pieces of silver (Zech 11:12). This was fulfilled when Judas betrayed Jesus for this exact amount as recorded in Matthew 26:15.

6. Isaiah prophesied that the Messiah would be rejected,

wounded and bruised for our sins and led like a lamb to the slaughter (see the 53rd chapter of Isaiah for details). These prophecies all came true in the life of Christ as one can see by reading Luke chapter 23.

7. Isaiah also predicted that the Messiah would be assigned a grave with wicked men, but that actually he would finally be buried in a rich man's tomb (Isaiah 53:9). And so it was in Jesus' case. The soldiers would have 'buried' Him with the two crucified criminals, but before they could do so, two prominent Jews, members of the Jewish Sanhedrin, Rabbi Nicodemus and Joseph of Arimathea, stepped forward and buried Jesus in a rich man's tomb (Matthew 27:57-60).

8. King David prophesied that the Messiah's body would not corrupt after death (Psalm 16:10). David knew that the Messiah would be raised up to sit on His throne and therefore would have to be resurrected. David's body corrupted - so the reference must be to David's greater Son, the Messiah. Since Jesus rose from the dead this verse finds its fulfilment only in Him (Acts 2:29-32).

If you think these 8 prophecies are incredible, further research will reveal that there are actually around 300 prophecies of this nature written in the Hebrew scriptures that were fulfilled in the life, death and resurrection of Jesus.

But was it possible that Jesus fulfilled these scriptures by accident? Was it merely a long string of coincidences? No. These prophecies are so detailed and specific that they could only ever be fulfilled in the life of one person. For instance, there are only a small number of people who have ever been born in Bethlehem, who were also crucified, who also lived before AD 70, who also were buried in a rich man's tomb. Each new prophecy makes the

43

scenario more fantastic. Professor Peter Stoner stated; "*We find th* *chance that any man might have lived down to the present time and fulfilled a* *eight prophecies is 1 in 10^{17}...That would be 1 in 100,000,000,000,000* *000*" (Peter W. Stoner, Science Speaks, Chicago: Moody Press 1969, p. 109). What would the odds be of one man fulfilling over 300 minutely detailed prophecies! Upon examination, the idea of mere coincidence is found wanting.

But what if the gospel writers, Matthew, Mark, Luke and John, fabricated or manipulated the details to make it look as if Jesus fulfilled the prophecies? Or perhaps Jesus just read the Jewish scriptures and engineered their fulfilment. While a case might be made for a few prophecies, this argument will not hold water as a whole. For example, how can you engineer who your mother will be and where and when you will be born? How can you engineer the actions of your enemies to, for example, stop them breaking your legs, once you are dead?

If the gospel record written by Matthew, Mark, Luke and John had been a fabrication, why were they willing to die for what they wrote and believed? Thousands of ordinary people have died for what they believed to be true, even though it was a lie. However, no one dies for something they *know to be false because they themselves made it up*, especially when they have a chance to recant and escape death by simply admitting to their fabrication. All twelve disciples of Jesus were severely persecuted for claiming Jesus rose from the dead. In fact, eleven of them were killed for persistently preaching this fact. If they had merely stolen the body out of the tomb and made up a myth about a resurrection, they would have owned up to their deliberate hoax in order to avoid death. There was no money in it for them - only martyrdom.

In any case, any falsification of the facts of the case would have been exposed immediately by living Romans and Jews who had witnessed the crucifixion. Although the Talmud refers to Jesus in derogatory ways, it never once claims that Jesus fabricated the fulfilment of Messianic prophecies.

So, what if Jesus is the Messiah? Then He is God's answer to humanity's problems, the greatest of which is sin. The Hebrew scriptures plainly state that we are all sinners (Isaiah 53:6, 59:2). Despite having the law, the festivals and all the glorious trappings of Judaism, individual Jewish people are no different to individual Gentiles in this respect - they have all sinned and come short of God's glory. Stealing, committing adultery and lying are equally sinful for both Jews and Gentiles. All have broken God's 10 Commandments and stand guilty before his holy law. How can our sins be atoned for? The law of God tells us: *"It is the blood that makes an atonement for the soul"* (Leviticus 17:11). God demands a sacrifice for sin. A sinless and holy blood substitute must die to satisfy the demands of God's holy law against our sin.

That's why the Messiah came. When Jesus died on the cross he was paying the price for sin - He was submitting to the punishment that was due - the death penalty. Although Jesus was sinless, He volunteered to accept the blame for our sins and to take the place of sinners on the cross. His blood atones for sin. He is the fulfilment of the Passover and all the sacrifices of the Sinai covenant which could never take away sin. Our good deeds and merits cannot save us, but Jesus' one offering has provided a way back to God. As it is appointed to us all to die once and face the judgment, so Jesus was once offered on the cross to bear the sins of the guilty so that they could be made righteous in God's sight. It is all so wonderfully true.

But how may I obtain the benefits of Jesus' one sacrifice? You must repent (turn from your sin) come to Him by faith and receive Him as your Lord and Saviour. If you can see your guilt and how you have offended the God of your fathers, look at the Lord Jesus on the cross. Just as Moses lifted up a copper snake on a pole in the desert (Numbers 21:8) as a cure for the snake-bitten Israelites - if they would simply do as they were commanded and look at it - so in looking by faith to the Lord Jesus Christ lifted up on the tree and believing that He is the Son of God who loved you and died for you, you, a repentant sinner, will receive everlasting life and peace with God.

Paul the Pharisee, who sat at the feet of the great Rabbi Gamaliel in the first century AD, wrote the following words: "*If you will confess with your mouth Jesus as Lord and believe in your heart that God has raised Him from the dead, you will be saved...for there is no difference between the Jew and the Greek, for the same Lord over all is rich unto all that call upon Him. For whoever calls on the name of the Lord shall be saved*" (Romans 10:9-13). Will you repent and trust solely in the Lord Jesus today?

Here, in summary, is an 9-point outline of the way of salvation from the Hebrew scriptures:

1. God demands that we are as holy as He is (Lev 19:2).
2. We, on the other hand, are all sinners (Ecc 7:20).
3. We are therefore separated from God (Isa 59:2).
4. We must turn from our sin in true repentance (Isa 55:7)
5. Our good works and self effort cannot save us (Isa 64:6).
6. Sin can only be atoned for by blood (Lev 17:11).
7. The true atonement was made by the Messiah (Isa 53).
8. Knowing the Messiah as Lord and Saviour brings forgiveness (Isa 43:25, Jer 31:31-34).
9. God gives His Holy Spirit to believers to enable them to live a new life for Him (Eze 36:26-27).

Since this book has referred to Isaiah chapter 53 so many

times and it is undoubtedly the most powerful Messianic passage in the Hebrew scriptures, it is reproduced here in full:

ISAIAH Chapter 53

"Who has believed our report? And to whom has the arm of the LORD been revealed? For He shall grow up before Him as a tender plant and as a root out of dry ground. He has no form or comeliness; and when we see Him, there is no beauty that we should desire Him. He is despised and rejected by men, a man of sorrows and acquainted with grief - and we hid, as it were, our faces from Him; He was despised, and we esteemed Him not. Surely He has borne our griefs and carried our sorrows; yet we esteemed Him stricken, smitten by God and afflicted. But He was wounded for our transgressions, He was bruised for our iniquities; the punishment for our peace was upon Him and by His stripes we are healed. Like sheep we have all gone astray; we have turned, every one, to his own way; and the LORD has laid on Him the iniquity of us all. He was oppressed and He was afflicted, yet He opened not His mouth; He was led as a lamb to the slaughter, and as a sheep before its shearers is silent, so He opened not His mouth. He was taken from prison and from judgment, and who will declare His generation? For He was cut off from the land of the living; for the transgressions of my people He was stricken. And He made His grave with the wicked and with the rich at His death, because He had done no violence, nor was any deceit in His mouth. Yet it pleased the LORD to bruise Him; He has put Him to grief. When You make His soul an offering for sin, He shall see His seed, He shall prolong His days, and the pleasure of the LORD shall prosper in His hand. He shall see the labour of His soul, and shall be satisfied. By His knowledge My righteous servant shall justify many, for He shall bear their iniquities. Therefore I will divide Him a portion with the great, and He shall divide the spoil with the strong, because He poured out His soul unto death, and He was numbered with the transgressors, and He bore the sin of many and made intercession for the transgressors."

But what weight does Isaiah 53 carry with the Rabbis? Do they believe it actually refers to the Messiah? Here are four interesting quotations by Rabbis concerning this great chapter:

"The Messiah - what is his name? The Rabbis said: 'His name is the Leper Scholar as it is written [in Isaiah 53:4] *'surely he hath born our grief and carried our sorrows. Yet we did esteem him a leper, smitten of God and afflicted'."* (The Babylonian Talmud: Sanhedrin 98b).

"Our Rabbis of blessed memory with one voice accept and affirm the opinion that the prophet [Isaiah] *is speaking of the King Messiah, and we ourselves shall also adhere to the same view."* (Commentary on Isaiah chapter 53 by Rabbi Moshe El-Sheik of Safed; a disciple of Joseph Caro, the author of the Shuchan Aruch. Commentaries on the Earlier Prophets).

"Likewise, said Isaiah, that He [Messiah] *would appear without acknowledging father or mother, 'He grew up before Him as a tender plant and as a shoot out of a dry ground (Isaiah 53:2)'."* (Maimonides 1135-1204).

"Forthwith the Holy One began to make a covenant with the Messiah: 'O Messiah, my righteousness', said he, 'The iniquities of those who are hidden beside Thee will cause Thee to enter into a hard yoke...' said the Messiah, 'Lord of the world I accept it joyfully, and will endure these chastisements...' Messiah accepted the chastisements of love, as it is written: 'He was oppressed, and He was afflicted [Isaiah 53:7]'."* (Rabbi Moshe Ha-Darshan, 10th and 11th centuries, Midrash on Bereshit).

May the reading of these life stories and the scriptures quoted be a great blessing to you. We trust you will find true peace in the Messiah who loved you and died for you two thousand years ago. He is a risen living Saviour, ready able and willing to save all who come unto God through Him. Will you take that step of faith right now and believe on the Lord Jesus Christ? Repent therefore and believe the gospel that your sins may be blotted out.

If, through reading this book, you have trusted Messiah Jesus as your Lord & Saviour you should immediately:

1) Thank Him for what He has done for you and ask yourself the question, *"What can I now do for Him?"*

2) Start speaking daily to Him in prayer from your heart, bringing Him praise and thanksgiving, as well as asking Him for blessings.

3) Get a Bible and start reading and studying it. Ask God to give you understanding on how to apply it practically to your life.

4) Find a group of Bible-believers and meet with them regularly.

5) Tell others what the Lord has done for you.

If you would like confidential help or further information, please feel free to contact us. We can supply you with free literature and details of a group of believers in your area. Our address is:

ACKNOWLEDGEMENTS

Walking back to Happiness - By kind permission of Helen Shapiro
Betrayed - By kind permission of Stan Telchin
Holocaust, Forbidden Book & My Search - Kind permission of the publisher Sean O'Sullivan, P.O. Box 7848, Johannesburg, South Africa, editor of the *Good News Magazine*.

Also available:

Dawn of the New Age	*5 New Agers Relate Their Search for the Truth*
Angels of Light	*5 Spiritualists Test the Spirits*
Messiah	*5 Jewish People Make The Greatest Discovery*
They Thought They Were Saved	*5 Christians Recall a Startling Discovery*
The Pilgrimage	*5 Muslims Make the Greatest Discovery*
Light Seekers	*5 Hindus Search for God*
Witches and Wizards	*5 Witches Find Eternal Wisdom*
Many Ways to God?	*5 Religious Leaders Discover the Truth*

Available from bookshops or direct from the publishers.

Published by:
John Ritchie Ltd.
40 Beansburn, Kilmarnock, Ayrshire, KA3 1RL.
Tel: + 44 (0) 1563 536394
Fax: + 44 (0) 1563 571191
Email: sales@johnritchie.co.uk
Web: www.ritchiechristianmedia.co.uk

Copyright: John Ritchie Ltd., 2012
ISBN: 978-1-900742-10-8